# Bill of Rights

**Written by Douglas M. Rife**

**Illustrated by Bron Smith**

## Teaching & Learning Company

1204 Buchanan St., P.O. Box 10
Carthage, IL 62321-0010

## This book belongs to

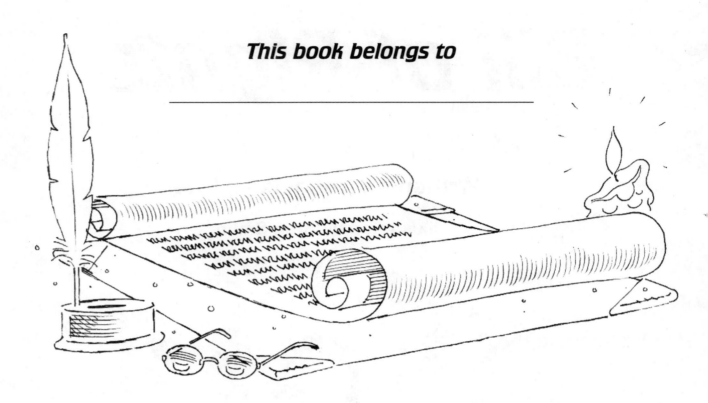

_____

Cover photo © 1988 Flag Research Center, Winchester, MA 01890

Copyright © 1997, Teaching & Learning Company

ISBN No. 1-57310-079-X

Printing No. 9876

**Teaching & Learning Company**
**1204 Buchanan St., P.O. Box 10**
**Carthage, IL 62321-0010**

# Table of Contents

# Dear Teacher or Parent,

Even before the Constitution was adopted by all of the states, the debate began for a bill of rights that would guarantee personal liberties and freedoms for the citizens of the newly formed country. In a letter, written on December 20, 1787, only three months after the Constitution was agreed upon by Congress to be sent to the states for ratification, Thomas Jefferson wrote to James Madison, "Let me add that a bill of rights is what the people are entitled to against every government on earth, general or particular, and what no government should refuse, or rest on inference."

The rights guaranteed in the Bill of Rights safeguard many of the freedoms that the colonists fought for in the Revolutionary War. Many of the freedoms that are guaranteed in the Bill of Rights were listed as grievances in the Declaration of Independence against King George III. The activities will help students put the Bill of Rights in an historical context.

The study of the Bill of Rights is important for students because it begins to give them a foundation in understanding what their rights are as citizens. The study of the Bill of Rights is relevant today because new generations must decide its meaning in the context of new technologies and an ever-changing world. Each generation decides what is cruel and unusual punishment, every generation decides what limits should be put on government. The Bill of Rights gives Americans the framework for safeguarding personal freedom against an oppressive government.

The activities in this book are to help students understand the Bill of Rights, the origins of those rights and the motivation of the framers of the first ten amendments to secure those freedoms.

Sincerely,

Douglas M. Rife

# Objectives

| After completing the following activities | the students should be able to . . . |
|---|---|
| **Ratification of the Constitution**<br>**Political Cartoons**<br>**Centinel Cartoon**<br>**Cartoon Questions** | 1. identify events leading up to the ratification of the Constitution<br>2. interpret the main idea of a political cartoon |
| **Bill of Rights Time Line** | 1. identify the authors of the Bill of Rights<br>2. understand the process to amend the Constitution |
| **Bill of Rights: Words to Look For**<br>**The Bill of Rights**<br>**The Bill of Rights Explained**<br>**Rights Review**<br>**Understanding the Bill of Rights**<br>**Who Said?** | 1. identify the historical reasons the framers wanted a bill of rights<br>2. explain the origins of the rights found in the first 10 amendments<br>3. identify the rights listed in the Bill of Rights<br>4. explain what the 10 amendments mean<br>5. explain the role of the Supreme Court |
| **Ladue City Ordinance**<br>**Englehardt's Cartoon**<br>**Ladue v. Gilleo**<br>**Ladue v. Gilleo Review**<br>**H.R. 1025, The Brady Bill**<br>**Brady Bill Review**<br>**Amendment II**<br>**Rights Review** | 1. define *freedom of speech*<br>2. understand speech in the context of signage<br>3. define *the right to bear arms*<br>4. understand limitations on right<br>5. understand a bill written by Congress<br>6. interpret political cartoons<br>7. draw conclusions<br>8. relate the Bill of Rights to real-life situations |

# Ratification of the Constitution

The Constitutional Convention in Philadelphia was finished on September 17, 1787. Copies of the Constitution were then sent to each of the 13 states for their ratification. Each of the 13 states then held conventions to decide on ratification of the Constitution. Delegates in each state were sent to conventions to vote on whether or not their state would ratify or vote for the Constitution to be the new law of the land, replacing the Articles of Confederation.

Below is a chart that shows the dates of ratification, when the vote was taken and what the tallies were for and against for each of the original 13 states.

| State | Date | For | Against |
|---|---|---|---|
| 1. Delaware | December 7, 1787 | 30 | 0 |
| 2. Pennsylvania | December 12, 1787 | 46 | 23 |
| 3. New Jersey | December 18, 1787 | 38 | 0 |
| 4. Georgia | January 2, 1788 | 26 | 0 |
| 5. Connecticut | January 4, 1788 | 128 | 40 |
| 6. Massachusetts | February 6, 1788 | 187 | 168 |
| 7. Maryland | April 28, 1788 | 63 | 11 |
| 8. South Carolina | May 23, 1788 | 149 | 73 |
| 9. New Hampshire | June 21, 1788 * | 57 | 47 |
| 10. Virginia | June 25, 1788 | 89 | 79 |
| 11. New York | July 26, 1788 | 30 | 27 |
| 12. North Carolina | November 21, 1789 | 195 | 77 |
| 13. Rhode Island | June 7, 1790 | 34 | 32 |

*The Constitution went into effect.

# Political Cartoons

The cartoon, "The Federal Edifice," was published August 2, 1788, by the Massachusetts *Centinel*.

## Words to Look For

**Redeunt Saturnia Regna**   Latin meaning "Return the Age of Saturn" or "Return Saturn's Regin"

**Saturnian**   Of Saturn, the Roman mythological god of agriculture whose reign was called the golden age

**Columbia**   A mythical figure who represents the United States, almost always in the form of a woman, named after Christopher Columbus

**Note:** When you read newspapers and pamphlets from 18th century America, notice that the small or lowercase *s* looks like an *f*. In the first line of the poem, it reads, "ELEVEN STARS, in quick succession rise–" not ELEVEN STARS, in quick fucceffion rife.

Below is the text of the poem.

## The FEDERAL EDIFICE

ELEVEN STARS, in quick succession rise–
ELEVEN COLUMNS strike our wond'ring eyes,
Soon o'er the *whole*, shall swell the beauteous DOME,
COLUMBIA's boast–and FREEDOM's hallow'd home.
   Here shall the ARTS in glorious splendour shine!
And AGRICULTURE give her shores divine!
COMMERCE refin'd dispense us more than gold,
And this new world, teach WISDOM to the old–
RELIGION here shall fix her blest abode,
Array'd in *mildness*, like its parent GOD!
JUSTICE and LAW, shall endless PEACE maintain,
And *the* "SATURNIAN AGE," *return again*.

REDEUNT SATURNIA REGNA.

*On the erection of the Eleventh PILLAR of the great National DOME, we beg leave most sincerely to felicitate " OUR DEAR COUNTRY "*

Rise it will.

N.CARO.

The foundation good——it may yet be SAVED.

N.YORK. VIRG. N.HAMP. S.CARO. MARY. MASSA. CON. GEOR. N.JER. PEN. DEL.

### The FEDERAL EDIFICE.

ELEVEN STARS, in quick succession rise—
ELEVEN COLUMNS strike our wond'ring eyes,
Soon o'er the *whole*, shall swell the beauteous DOME,
COLUMBIA's boast—and FREEDOM's hallow'd home.
Here shall the ARTS in glorious splendour shine !
And AGRICULTURE give her stores divine !
COMMERCE refin'd, dispense us more than gold,
And this new world, teach WISDOM to the old—
RELIGION here shall fix her blest abode,
Array'd in *mildness*, like its parent GOD !
JUSTICE and LAW, shall endless PEACE maintain,
And *the* " SATURNIAN AGE," *return again.*

Name _____

## Massachusetts Centinel

# "The Federal Edifice" Cartoon Questions

Study the cartoon published by the Massachusetts *Centinel*. Read the chart listing the ratification dates of the Constitution at state conventions and answer the questions below.

1. What does each of the pillars represent? _____

2. What is the significance to the order of the pillars? _____

   _____

3. Look up *metaphor* in the dictionary. Explain how the cartoon uses metaphor.

   _____

   _____

4. Who is Columbia? _____

5. What is the "Saturnian Age"? _____

6. List five things that the poem predicts will happen if all 13 pillars are erected? _____

   _____

   _____

7. Is the cartoonist in favor or against ratification of the Constitution? Explain your answer.

   _____

   _____

8. Which two states had the closest vote on ratification?

   _____

9. Which three states ratified the Constitution by unanimous vote?

   _____

10. How many states did it take for the ratification of the Constitution? _____

**Trick Question:** Was the ratification of the Constitution unanimous? _____

**Bonus Question:** What is Delaware's nickname and how did it get that name?

_____

# Bill of Rights Time Line

**September 17, 1787:** The Constitution is completed and signed in Philadelphia at the Pennsylvania State House and sent to the states for ratification. The framers had debated how amendments could be added to the new Constitution during the May to September convention. There had been debate about adding a Bill of Rights even before the Constitution was finished.

George Mason of Virginia had offered to write a bill of rights. He deeply distrusted powerful, centralized and autocratic government and believed that individual rights had to be protected. Though Mason had authored the Virginia Bill of Rights, the delegates voted down his proposal. Mason was so upset that the document did not include a bill of rights that he would not sign the completed Constitution. ARTICLE V of the Constitution, however, gave future generations a way to amend the document and assured that the debate and push for a bill of rights would continue.

**June 21, 1788:** New Hampshire ratifies the Constitution and the Constitution goes into effect. The new government begins to take shape.

**April 1, 1789:** The first House of Representatives is organized.

**April 6, 1789:** George Washington is elected President. He is greeted by cheering crowds from Virginia to New York. Washington is the most celebrated American of his time.

**April 30, 1789:** George Washington is inaugurated as the first President of the United States of America. He takes the oath of office, required by the Constitution, on the balcony of the Federal Building in New York City.

**June 8, 1789:** James Madison, Congressman from Virginia, in the new House of Representatives offers amendments to the Constitution.

**September 25, 1789:** Congress submits 12 amendments to the Constitution to the states for ratification. Only 10 are approved by the states at the state convention, these 10 become known as the "Bill of Rights." The states hold conventions to ratify the Bill of Rights. The following states ratify the Bill of Rights:

| 1. New Jersey | November 20, 1789 | 6. New York | February 27, 1790 |
| 2. Maryland | December 19, 1789 | 7. Pennsylvania | March 10, 1790 |
| 3. North Carolina | December 22, 1789 | 8. Rhode Island | June 7, 1790 |
| 4. New Hampshire | January 25, 1790 | 9. Vermont* | November 3, 1791 |
| 5. Delaware | January 28, 1790 | 10. Virginia | December 15, 1791 |

*On January 10, 1791, though not yet a state, Vermont ratifies the Constitution. Vermont is admitted into the Union on March 4, 1791, as the fourteenth state.*

Name _____

# Understanding the Events Leading up to the Bill of Rights

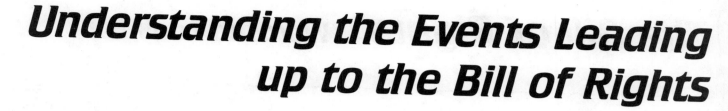

1. Who is called the Father of the Bill of Rights? _____

2. How many states did it take to ratify the Bill of Rights? _____

3. Was the ratification of the Bill of Rights unanimous? _____

4. Where did the Congress derive its power to amend the Constitution? Research this in the Constitution; explain what the document says. _____

_____

_____

_____

**Extra Credit:** Draw your own political cartoon in the box below in favor of the ratification of the Bill of Rights.

# The Bill of Rights: Words to Look For

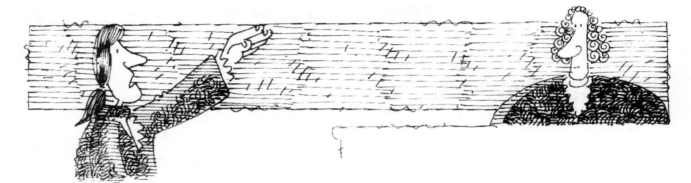

**bail**      Money deposited with the court to get an arrested person temporarily released from jail on a promise to appear for trial

**capital crime**      Crimes punishable by death, such as murder or treason

**common law**      Laws dealing with private, not criminal or military, matters

**due process**      The legal proceedings established by a nation or state to protect individual rights and liberties

**disparage**      To discredit

**enumeration**      Determining the number of, the count

**grievance**      A situation thought unjust and reason for compliant and remedy

**indictment**      A formal accusation by a grand jury, charging a person with a crime after studying the evidence

**infamous crime**      Punishable by imprisonment

**infringed**      To encroach, or trespass

**jeopardy**      To place a person in great danger or peril

**oath**      A declaration to keep a promise or to tell the truth

**petition**      A written request or plea in which specific court action is requested

**redress**      To set right, often by making compensation for a wrong

**seizure**      The act of legally taking possession by force

**warrant**      A court order giving an officer legal authority to make an arrest, seizure or search

**writ**      A formal legal document ordering or prohibiting some action

# The Bill of Rights

**AMENDMENT I**  Congress shall make no law respecting an establishment of religion, or prohibiting the free exercise thereof; or abridging the freedom of speech, or of the press, or the right of the people peaceably to assemble, and to petition the Government for a redress of grievances.

**AMENDMENT II**  A well regulated Militia, being necessary to the security of a free State, the right of the people to keep and bear Arms, shall not be infringed.

**AMENDMENT III**  No soldier shall, in time of peace be quartered in any house, without the consent of the Owner, nor in times of war, but in a manner to be prescribed by law.

**AMENDMENT IV**  The right of the people to be secure in their persons, houses, papers, and effects, against unreasonable searches and seizures, shall not be violated, and no Warrants shall issue, but upon probable cause, supported by Oath or affirmation, and particularly describing the place to be searched, and the persons or things to be seized.

**AMENDMENT V**  No person shall be held to answer for a capital, or otherwise infamous crime, unless on a presentment or indictment of a Grand Jury, except in cases arising in the land or naval forces, or in the Militias, when in actual service in time of War or public danger; nor shall any person be subject for the same offence to be twice put in jeopardy of life or limb, nor shall be compelled in any criminal case to be a witness against himself, nor be deprived of life, liberty, or property be taken for public use without just compensation.

**AMENDMENT VI**   In all criminal prosecutions, the accused shall enjoy the right to a speedy public trial, by an impartial jury of the State and district wherein the crime shall have been committed; which district shall have been previously ascertained by law, and to be informed of the nature and cause of the accusation; to be confronted with the witnesses against him; to have compulsory process for obtaining witnesses in his favor, and to have the assistance of counsel for his defence.

**AMENDMENT VII**   In suits at common law, where the value in controversy shall exceed twenty dollars, the right of trial by jury shall be preserved, and no fact tried by a jury shall be otherwise re-examined in any Court of the United States, than according to the rules of the common law.

**AMENDMENT VIII**   Excessive bail shall not be required, nor excessive fines imposed, nor cruel and unusual punishments inflicted.

**AMENDMENT IX**   The enumeration in the Constitution of certain rights shall not be construed to deny or disparage others retained by the people.

**AMENDMENT X**   The powers not delegated to the United States by the Constitution, nor prohibited by it to the States, are reserved to the States respectively, or to the people.

# The Bill of Rights Explained

## AMENDMENT I.

*Congress shall make no law respecting an establishment of religion, or prohibiting the free exercise there-of; or abridging the freedom of speech, or of the press, or the right of the people peaceably to assemble, and to petition the Government for a redress of grievances.*

This is perhaps the most important amendment to the Constitution. It protects five basic rights from intrusion by the government—religion, speech, press, assembly and redress of grievances.

The first part of the First Amendment protects the freedom of religion. The First Amendment protects religion in two ways. First, by keeping the government from establishing a state religion. This is called "The Establishment Clause." It simply means that the government cannot pass laws to favor one religion over another. Congress cannot make one religion the religion of the country. Secondly, this amendment protects religion by allowing people to practice any religion they choose. This is referred to as "The Free Exercise Clause." Though Congress cannot pass laws curbing anyone's rights to believe anything they want, it can legislate to stop certain religious practices. For instance, Congress prohibits the practice of polygamy.

The second part of the First Amendment protects citizens' right to speak freely. Benjamin Franklin said, "Whoever would overthrow the liberty of a nation must begin by subduing the freeness of speech." The people who wrote the Bill of Rights believed this to be a most basic human right.

This right, too, has limitations. Speech can be limited if there is "a clear and present danger." In 1919, the Supreme Court case Schenck v. United States, the Supreme Court ruled that Schenck had distributed leaflets to men to encourage them to resist the draft. The government convicted Schenck under the Espionage Act. Schenck maintained that freedom of speech entitled him to be able to say whatever he wished. The court ruled "We admit that in many places and in ordinary times the defendants, in saying all that was said in the circular, would have been within their constitutional rights. But the character of every act depends upon the circumstances in which it is done ... The most stringent protection of free speech would not protect a man in falsely shouting fire in a theater, and causing a panic ... The question in every case is whether the words used are in such circumstances and are of such a nature as to create a **clear and present danger** ... When a nation is at war, many things that might be said in time of peace are such a hindrance to its effort that their utterances will not be endured so long as men fight, and that no Court could regard them as protected by any constitutional right."

The First Amendment also guarantees the freedom of the press. In a letter to Colonel Edward Carrington (January 16, 1787) Thomas Jefferson wrote, "Were it left to me to decide whether we should have a government without newspapers, or newspapers without a government, I should not hesitate a moment to prefer the latter." Jefferson and others knew and believed that a free and independent press was necessary in a democracy. The authors of the Virginia Bill of Rights recognized this when they wrote, "That the freedom of the press is one of the great bulwarks of liberty and can never be restrained but by despotick governments." But can the press print anything it wants to? No. There are restrictions on the press just as there are restrictions on the freedom of speech. The same test of "clear and present danger" applies to the press.

The right of the people to peaceably assemble gives people the right to gather and discuss, protest or march in favor of whatever subjects they choose. This right dates back to the revolutionary period in America and was specifically guaranteed by the Pennsylvania Declaration of Rights of 1776.

However, the court, in Cox v. Louisiana (1965), has stated that it would not allow "demonstrations, however, peaceful or commendable their motives, which conflict with properly drawn statutes and ordinances designed to promote law and order, protect the community against disorder, regulate traffic, safeguard legitimate interests in private and public property, or protect the administration of justice and other essential Governmental functions." So, even though people have the right to protest and assemble in groups to do so, they still need to be mindful of regulations governing it. These include federal and state laws and local ordinances.

The last of the five activities protected in the First Amendment is the right to "petition the Government for a redress of grievances." This has long since been considered a right. It was protected under the English Bill of Rights of 1689. This simply means that a person has the right to circulate a piece of paper and gather names of people who agree with you that the government has done something wrong that you want to be fixed or righted.

# AMENDMENT II.

*A well regulated Militia, being necessary to the security of a free State, the right of the people to keep and bear Arms, shall not be infringed.*

The smoke from the muskets that rousted the British from American shores had barely cleared when the framers wrote this amendment. The Revolutionary War was still fresh in their minds. It had been Minute Men and citizen militias, along with a ragtag Continental Army that had defeated the British. The framers wanted to protect citizens and their right to carry guns and safeguard the people against a government that was too strong. Only an armed citizenry could do that. This right, had been the right of the protestant Englishmen since the English Bill of Rights of 1689, "the subjects, which are protestants, may have arms for their defence suitable to their conditions, and as allowed by law."

Just as the English Bill of Rights put restrictions on gun ownership, so, too, does Congress. The Supreme Court ruled in U.S. v. Miller (1939) that the federal government could ban certain kinds of weapons. Other restrictions have been applied as well, such as waiting periods, permits, training and gun safety classes.

However, organizations such as the National Rifle Association (NRA) argue that the Second Amendment protects all gun ownership. The NRA is a powerful lobby group that works at the local, state and national level for less restrictive gun laws. This debate continues.

## AMENDMENT III.

*No soldier shall, in time of peace be quartered in any house, without the consent of the Owner, nor in times of war, but in a manner to be prescribed by law.*

This amendment probably doesn't seem like much to worry about now, but from 1765 until the end of the American Revolution, British troops were stationed in the colonies. Various laws were passed to force the colonists to provide lodging and provisions for the soldiers. On March 28, 1774, Parliament passed the Quartering Act. This measure provided that the British troops that were stationed in Boston at that time could be housed in private citizens' homes, in inns and in public warehouses. The American colonists were outraged.

When Thomas Jefferson wrote the Declaration of Independence, "quartering large bodies of armed troops among us" was listed among the grievances against King George III. The Americans had not forgotten the tyranny of the king reaching all the way into their own homes. The framers made sure this would not happen again by the new government they were creating.

In 1833, Justice Joseph Story summed up the Third Amendment when he wrote, "This provision speaks for itself. Its plain objective is to secure the perfect enjoyment of that great right of the common law, that a man's house shall be his own castle, privileged against all civil and military intrusion."

# AMENDMENT IV.

*The right of the people to be secure in their persons, houses, papers, and effects, against unreasonable searches and seizures, shall not be violated, and no Warrants shall issue, but upon probable cause, supported by Oath or affirmation, and particularly describing the place to be searched, and the persons or things to be seized.*

Under a series of laws passed in 1767, Parliament gave broad powers to British customs officers and their subordinates who were searching homes and commercial buildings for smuggled goods. The officers were given *writs of assistance*, giving them permission to search any houses they chose, anytime, for any reason. Not only could these customs officers search any house they wished, the writs of assistance were transferable to their assistants.

James Otis was a fiery orator in the American colonies and an able advocate for civil liberties. Otis was asked to argue for the Boston merchants against the customs officers holding the writs. Though, Otis lost the case, he eloquently outlined the elements that should be found in a writ to safeguard people against an abuse of civil authority.

"I will admit that writs of one kind may be legal; that is special writs, directed to special officers and to search certain houses, specially set forth in the writ, may be granted by the Court . . . upon oath made before the Lord Treasurer by the person who asks it, that he suspects such goods to be concealed in those very places he desires to search . . . one of the most essential branches of English liberty is the freedom of one's house. A man's house is his castle; and whilst he is quiet, he is as well guarded as a prince in his castle . . . I before observed, that special writs may be granted on oath and probable suspicion . . . that an officer should show probable ground; should take his oath of it; should do this before a magistrate; and that such magistrate, if he thinks proper, should issue a special warrant to a constable to search the places."

James Otis laid out his case against writs of assistance. The very elements that he believed should guide the law in issuing warrants for search and seizure can be found in the Fourth Amendment.

# AMENDMENT V.

*No person shall be held to answer for a capital, or otherwise infamous crime, unless on a presentment or indictment of a Grand Jury, except in cases arising in the land or naval forces, or in the Militias, when in actual service in time of War or public danger; nor shall any person be subject for the same offence to be twice put in jeopardy of life or limb, nor shall be compelled in any criminal case to be a witness against himself, nor be deprived of life, liberty, or property be taken for public use without just compensation.*

This amendment has three main clauses. The first clause guarantees that, except in military cases, no one can be held in jail for a crime that is punishable by death or imprisonment, unless a Grand Jury evaluates the evidence presented to it and determines that there is enough evidence for a trial. (A Grand Jury is made up of 12 or more people.)

The second clause contains three parts. The **first** says a person cannot be tried for the same crime twice. Once you are found not guilty by a jury, you cannot be tried for that crime again. The **second** says a defendant does not have to testify against himself. In the Supreme Court case Miranda v. Arizona, the court said that, "Prior to any questioning, the person must be warned that he has a right to remain silent, that any statement he does make may be used as evidence against him, and that he has a right to the presence of an attorney, either retained or appointed. The defendant may waive effectuation of these rights provided the wavier is made voluntarily, knowingly and intelligently. If, however, he indicates in any manner and at any stage of the process that he wishes to consult with an attorney before speaking, there can be no questioning." The **third** part of this clause has its roots in the Magna Carta of 1215. King John promised to give "due process of law" to all accused of crimes. All citizens are entitled to all courses of the law before the government can take away life, liberty, or property.

The third clause protects people and their property from the government. The government cannot take private property for public use, for instance to build a highway, without paying a fair market value to the owner.

## AMENDMENT VI.

*In all criminal prosecutions, the accused shall enjoy the right to a speedy public trial, by an impartial jury of the State and district wherein the crime shall have been committed; which district shall have been previously ascertained by law, and to be informed of the nature and cause of the accusation; to be confronted with the witnesses against him; to have compulsory process for obtaining witnesses in his favor, and to have the assistance of counsel for his defence.*

Many of the amendments in the Bill of Rights were born out of the experience of the American Revolution. This amendment is no exception. The king could send colonists to Canada or even as far as England to stand trial. The colonials believed that to be unjust and protested it in the Declaration of Independence when Jefferson wrote, "For transporting us beyond Seas to be tried for pretended offences."

As English subjects, the colonists believed they had a right to a speedy trial. The Magna Carta guaranteed, "No bailiff shall in future put anyone to trial upon his own bare word, without reliable witnesses produced for this purpose. No free man shall be arrested or imprisoned or outlawed or exiled or in any way victimized, neither will we attack him or send anyone to attack him, except by lawful judgement of his peers or by the law of the land."

Yet, during the colonial period of America, the colonists felt as if their rights as English citizens were not upheld. This amendment lays out eight specific rules for the judicial treatment of people who are charged with a crime. Anyone charged with a crime has a right to a speedy trial. The trial has to be public so nothing secret can go one unseen by the citizens. The jury has to be impartial or made up of people who do not have an opinion about the crime that had been committed or the accused. The trial has to take place in the place where the crime is committed. The accused has to be informed of the charges. The person on trial has to be able to see the people who were witnesses in the case. The accused had to have a means by which to call witnesses of his own defence. And lastly, the person accused of the crime has a right to an attorney.

## AMENDMENT VII.

*In suits at common law, where the value in controversy shall exceed twenty dollars, the right of trial by jury shall be preserved, and no fact tried by a jury shall be otherwise re-examined in any Court of the United States, than according to the rules of the common law.*

Amendments five and six deal with criminal cases, but this amendment pertains to civil cases. The framers believed in these cases, too, that citizens should be protected against oppressive government. The framers feared that government could use the court system to oppress people with heavy fines and arbitrary lawsuits.

To keep the court from harassing private citizens, this amendment guarantees trial by jury for cases involving more than 20 dollars. In 1791, when this amendment was ratified, 20 dollars represented about 40 days pay for the average American.

When the Seventh Amendment was written, the framers of the Bill of Rights saw the jury system as a safeguard against the government. Patrick Henry believed that the trial by jury, "prevented the hand of oppression from cutting you off."

# AMENDMENT VIII.

*Excessive bail shall not be required, nor excessive fines imposed, nor cruel and unusual punishments inflicted.*

Amendment Eight represents another safeguard in the Bill of Rights against overzealous and unreasonable treatment of citizens by the court. This amendment has its origins in the English Bill of Rights of 1689 and is taken from that document nearly word for word. "That excessive bail ought not to be required, nor excessive fines imposed; nor cruel and unusual punishment inflicted."

In Stack v. Boyle, Chief Justice Vinson defined what the Supreme Court meant by excessive bail. "The right to release before trial is conditioned upon the accused's giving adequate assurance that he will stand trial and submit to sentence if found guilty ... Like the ancient practice of securing the oaths of responsible persons to stand as sureties for the accused, the modern practice of requiring a bail bond or the deposit of a sum of money subject to forfeiture serves as additional assurance of the presence of an accused. Bail set at a figure higher than an amount reasonably calculated to fulfill this purpose is excessive under the Eighth Amendment."

The meaning of the term *cruel and unusual* has changed from one generation to another. At the time this amendment was written, the framers knew many punishments that we would now consider cruel and unusual. For instance, high treason in Great Britain was punishable by hanging. Then the person would be cut down and disemboweled, while still alive, have his head cut off, and his body cut into four parts. Other, much less severe punishments were common then, as well. A person could be sentenced to stand all day long in the stocks, a wooden frame made in two parts and hinged, so when it closed it fit around the neck and wrists. Part of the punishment was the discomfort of being in the stocks and not being able to move about and the humiliation of being seen this way in public. The punishment for some lesser crimes also included cutting or slitting the nostrils. All of these punishments would be considered cruel and unusual today.

## AMENDMENT IX.

*The enumeration in the Constitution of certain rights shall not be construed to deny or disparage others retained by the people.*

Justice William O. Douglas described the Ninth Amendment as protecting the "freedom of choice in the basic decisions of one's life respecting marriage, divorce, procreation, contraception, and the education and upbringing of children."

This amendment was born out of the fear the Americans had of tyrannical government. The colonists had just fought a long and costly war to rid themselves of the power of a king, they didn't want a new government to take the king's place. Why switch one tyrant for another?

The writers of the Bill of Rights feared that if the rights weren't spelled out in the Constitution, that the federal government would assume jurisdiction. This amendment was written to make sure that wouldn't happen.

## AMENDMENT X.

*The powers not delegated to the United States by the Constitution, nor prohibited by it to the States, are reserved to the States respectively, or to the people.*

The debate over who should have more power the states or the federal government was at the heart of the Constitutional Convention of 1787 and has and continues to this day. This amendment was written to guarantee that the federal government could not usurp power from the states by claiming powers not delegated to it by the Constitution.

Woodrow Wilson characterized the debate between federal and state powers this way, "This question of the relationship of the States to federal government is the cardinal question of our constitutional system. At every turn of our national development we have seen brought face to face with it, and no definition either of statesmen or of judges has ever quieted or decided it. It cannot, indeed be settled by the opinion of any one generation, because it is a question of growth, and every successive stage of our political and economic development gives it a new aspect, makes it a new question."

The Constitution leaves it to the states to make laws about marriage, divorce, education, zoning, public health, driving regulations, state roads, among others.

Name _____

# Rights Review

Place the amendment number next to the right guaranteed by the Bill of Rights.

_____ 1. The right to a trial by jury in criminal cases

_____ 2. The right to call witnesses in one's defence at a trial

_____ 3. Freedom of the press

_____ 4. Not to testify against oneself

_____ 5. The right to be informed of why you are being arrested

_____ 6. Freedom of religion

_____ 7. The right to a trial by jury in civil cases of $20.

_____ 8. No excessive bail

_____ 9. The right to bear arms

_____ 10. Protection from unreasonable search and seizure

_____ 11. Right to a speedy trial

_____ 12. Freedom of speech

_____ 13. No cruel or unusual punishment

_____ 14. The right to confront witnesses

_____ 15. The right not to quarter soldiers in your home

_____ 16. Cannot be tried for the same crime twice

_____ 17. The right to assembly

_____ 18. The right to a trial in the district the crime occurred.

_____ 19. Cannot be deprived of life, liberty, or property without just compensation

_____ 20. The right to redress of grievances

Name _____

# Understanding the Bill of Rights

Read the situations below. Then answer the questions. The answer to each question is in the Bill of Rights.

1. A man's religion expresses a belief in multiple marriage. As an expression of that religion, that man takes four wives. The state he lives in arrested him on a charge of polygamy. Doesn't he have the right to practice his religion?  Is the arrest legal?

   _____

   _____

2. The State of Iowa has designed an interstate highway to run through Mr. and Mrs. Schwertley's farm. The Schwertleys do not want to sell their land even though the state is paying them a fair market price for the land. Do they have to sell? (Hint: Look up *eminent domain*.)

   _____

   _____

3. In a celebrated case, a movie star is charged with murder. After a lengthy trial, the jury declares the actor "not guilty."  Several months after the trial is over, additional evidence is discovered that proves the actor committed the crime.  Can the actor be tried again?

   _____

   _____

4. A local animal rights organization doesn't like the city's dog leash ordinance. The organization coordinates a protest march, making sure their permits are in order. The day of the march, the leader is jailed.  Is the arrest legal?

   _____

   _____

5. A man is caught stealing a loaf of bread from a local store.  He is arrested and convicted of the crime. The judge sentenced him to 30 days in jail and ordered that his right hand be cut off. The sentence was struck down. Why?

   _____

   _____

*Handout 11*                    TLC10079 Copyright © Teaching & Learning Company, Carthage, IL 62321-0010

Name _____

# Who Said?

Match the quote with the person who said it. Write the letter of the person who spoke or wrote the quote in the space next to the number. Underneath the quote, write the number of the amendment that the author of the quote was referring to.

_____ 1. "Freedom of choice in the basic decisions of one's life respecting marriage, divorce, pro-creation, contraception, and the education and upbringing of children."

_____

_____ 2. "Were it left to me to decide whether we should have a government without newspa-pers, or newspapers without a government, I should not hesitate a moment to prefer the latter."

_____

_____ 3. "Whoever would overthrow the liberty of a nation must begin by subduing the free-ness of speech."

_____

_____ 4. "A man's house is his castle; and whilst he is quiet, he is as well guarded as a prince in his castle."

_____

_____ 5. "Bail set at a figure higher than an amount reasonably calculated to fulfill this purpose is excessive."

_____

_____ 6. "It's plain objective is to secure the perfect enjoyment of that great right of the com-mon law, that a man's house shall be his own castle, privileged against all civil and military intrusion."

_____

A. James Otis

B. Thomas Jefferson

C. Justice Joseph Story

D. Benjamin Franklin

E. Justice William O. Douglas

F. Chief Justice Vinson

# The Bill of Rights in Action
# Exercising Your Rights

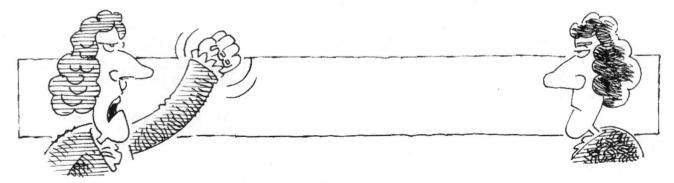

The following pages have activities that give students a look at two real-life debates over constitutional rights–the freedom of speech and the right to bear arms.

In the City of Ladue v. Gilleo, the student is provided with six reproducible handouts: Freedom of Speech: You Decide–Ladue v. Gilleo; Ladue Code; Political Cartoons; Cartoon Quiz; City of Ladue v. Gilleo Supreme Court Case; Ladue v. Gilleo Review. These exercises are designed to give the students a real-life view of the tug of war between the government's right to regulate and a person's right to freedom of expression, and how the Supreme Court balances the interests of both.

The second set of handouts–H.R.1025, The Brady Bill; Brady Bill Review; Engelhardt Cartoon; Amendment II–gives the students a firsthand look at the debate over how Congress can regulate the Second Amendment and how lobby groups view and interpret the power of the Second Amendment.

In both of these exercises the students are introduced to political cartoons as an editorial form. It is a good way to introduce topics and to begin discussion sessions. To further discussions, ask students to draw their own cartoons illustrating their views on the Brady Bill and the City of Ladue v. Gilleo freedom of speech case.

The Ladue v. Gilleo is also an opportunity to explain other kinds of speech that are protected, such as symbolic speech. For instance, burning an American flag, even though it is conduct, is considered symbolic speech and is protected by the First Amendment. Ask the students to explain how they feel about the flag burning amendment that has been proposed but never received enough votes to pass the Senate. Would they support the amendment? Should conduct be protected as speech?

**30**

# Freedom of Speech: You Decide—Ladue v. Gilleo

Below are the words from the First Amendment that protect freedom of speech and a brief description of the details of a case that went to the Supreme Court. Read both and form your own opinion of whether or not the City of Ladue, Missouri, violated Margaret Gilleo's right to free speech.

## Words to Look For

**Abridge**   to shorten, to lessen, to cut

**Respondent**   the defendant in a civil court proceeding

**Ordinance**   a municipal or city statute or law

**AMENDMENT I** **Congress shall make no law** respecting an establishment of religion, or prohibiting the free exercise thereof; **or abridging the freedom of speech**, or of the press, or the right of the people peaceably to assemble, and to petition the Government for a redress of grievances.

### City of Ladue v. Margaret P. Gilleo

"Respondent Margaret P. Gilleo owns one of the 57 single-family homes in the Willow Hill subdivision of Ladue, Missouri. On December 8, 1990, she placed on her front lawn a 24" x 36" sign printed with the words *Say No to War in the Persian Gulf, Call Congress Now!*. That sign disappeared. Gilleo put up another but it was knocked to the ground. When Gilleo reported these incidents to the police, they advised her that such signs were prohibited in Ladue. The City Council denied her petition for a variance. Gilleo then filed this action . . . against the City, the Mayor, and members of the City Council, alleging that Ladue's sign ordinance violated her First Amendment right to free speech."

# Political Cartoons

Political cartoons make their editorial comments through art rather than writing. Even though most political cartoons contain writing, most of the message is to be found in the art. The cartoonist relies on the reader to understand the message in the cartoon. For this to happen, the reader has to be familiar with the story and the events relating to the cartoon.

The cartoon below, drawn by Tom Engelhardt, was printed in the *St. Louis Post-Dispatch*, June 15, 1994.

'There Goes The Neighborhood!'

Reprinted with permission.

Name _____

# *Cartoon Quiz*

Study the cartoon and answer the following questions:

1. Is the house in the cartoon big or small? _____

2. What kind of car do you think the two people in the car are riding in? _____

3. Describe the expression on the face of the man driving the car. Is he happy or angry?

   _____

4. What does the new sign say in the front yard? _____

5. Do you think Margaret Gilleo won or lost her case? _____

   _____

   _____

6. Given all of the visual clues in the cartoon, how do you think the people feel about signs in

   their neighborhood? _____

   _____

7. Do you think the cartoonist agrees with the townspeople of Ladue? Why or why not?

   _____

   _____

## Further Discussion

Do you consider burning a flag to be speech or an act?

# City of Ladue v. Gilleo Supreme Court Case

**Date Argued:** February 23, 1994
**Opinion Date:** June 13, 1994

"While signs are a form of expression protected by the Free Speech Clause, they pose distinctive problems that are subject to municipalities' police powers. Unlike oral speech, signs take up space and obstruct views, distract motorists, displace alternative uses for land, and pose other problems that legitimately call for regulation. It is common ground that governments may regulate the physical characteristics of signs ... Ladue has almost completely foreclosed a venerable means of communication that is both unique and important. It has totally foreclosed that medium to political, religious, or personal messages ... Often placed on lawns or in windows, residential signs play an important part in political campaigns, during which they are displayed to signal the resident's support for particular candidates, parties or causes. They may not afford the same opportunities for conveying complex ideas as do other media, but residential signs have long been an important and distinct medium of expression ... Displaying a sign from one's own residence often carries a message quite distinct from placing the same sign someplace else, or conveying the same text or picture by other means. Precisely because of their location, such signs provide information about the identity of the 'speaker.'"

Residential signs are an unusually cheap and convenient form of communication . . . Furthermore, a person who puts up a sign at her residence often intends to reach neighbors, an audience that could not be reached nearly as well by other means.

A special respect for individual liberty in the home has long been part of our culture and our law ... Most Americans would be understandably dismayed, given that tradition, to learn that it was illegal to display from their window an 8" x 11" sign expressing their political views ...

Our decision that Ladue's ban on almost all residential signs violated the First Amendment ... We are confident that more temperate measures could in large part satisfy Ladue's stated regulatory needs without harm to the First Amendment rights of its citizens. As currently framed, however, the ordinance abridges those rights.

Accordingly, the judgement of the Court of Appeals is Affirmed.

## Sec. 35-4. Limited number and size of signs permitted.

Subject to the applicable regulation hereinafter described, the following types of signs are permitted in the city:

1. Municipal signs, but such signs shall not be greater than nine (9) square feet.

2. Subdivision and residence identification signs of a permanent character, but such subdivision identification signs shall not be greater than six (6) square feet, and such residence identification signs shall not be greater than one (1) square foot.

3. Road signs and driveway signs for danger, direction, or identification, but such signs shall not be greater than twelve (12) square feet.

4. Health inspection signs, but such signs shall not be greater than two (2) square feet.

5. Signs for churches, religious institutions, and schools subject to the restrictions described in section 35-5.

6. Identification signs for not-for-profit organizations not otherwise described herein, but such signs shall not be greater than sixteen (16) square feet.

7. Signs identifying the location of public transportation stops, but such signs shall not be greater than three (3) square feet.

8. Ground signs advertising the sales or rental of real property subject to the restrictions described in section 35-10.

9. Commercial signs in commercially zoned or industrial zoned districts subject to the restrictions as to size, location, and time of placement hereinafter described.

10. Signs identifying safety hazards, but such signs shall not be greater than twelve (12) square feet.

Name _____

# Ladue v. Gilleo Review

Say **NO** to war in
the Persian Gulf,
Call Congress
**NOW**!

1. How are signs different from oral speech? _____

   _____

   _____

2. What does the Supreme Court decision say about regulating signs? _____

   _____

   _____

   _____

3. What does *venerable* mean? _____

   _____

   _____

   _____

4. How is a sign from a yard or the window of a home significant?_____

   _____

   _____

   _____

5. List three qualities the Supreme Court decision ascribes to residential signs.

   _____

   _____

   _____

6. In the third paragraph, the decision says, "A special respect for individual liberty in the home
   has long been part of our culture and our law." Name two amendments to the Bill of Rights

   that protect the home from the government. _____

   _____

7. Do you agree with the Supreme Court decision? Explain. _____

   _____

   _____

   _____

# H.R.1025, The Brady Bill

## H.R. 1025, 103rd Congress, Washington, D.C., January 5, 1993

**An Act**

To provide for a waiting period before the purchase of a handgun, and for the establishment of a national instant criminal background check system to be conducted by firearms dealers before the transfer of any firearm.

*Be it enacted by the Senate and House of Representatives of the United States in Congress assembled,*

### BRADY HANDGUN CONTROL

...(1) ...it shall be unlawful for any licensed importer, licensed manufacturer, or licensed dealer to sell, deliver, or transfer a handgun to an individual who is not licensed ... unless—

(A) after the most recent proposal of such transfer by the transferee—(i) the transferor has—

(I) received from the transferee a statement of the transferee containing . . . (A) the name, address, and date of birth appearing on a valid identification document . . . of the transferee containing a photograph of the transferee and a description of the identification used; (B) a statement that the transferee—

  (i) is not under indictment for, and has not been convicted in any court of, a crime punishable by imprisonment for a term exceeding one year;

  (ii) is not a fugitive from justice;

  (iii) is not an unlawful user of or addicted to any controlled substance . . .

  (iv) has not been adjudicated as a mental defective or been committed to a mental institution;

  (v) is not an alien who is illegally or unlawfully in the United States;

  (vi) has not been discharged from the armed Forces under dishonorable conditions; and

  (vii) is not a person who, having been a citizen of the United States, has renounced such citizenship;

     *Handout 19*    

(II) ... examining the identification document presented;

(III) within one day after the transferee furnishes the statement, provided notice of the contents of the statement of the chief law enforcement officer of the place of residence of the transferee; and

(IV) within one day after the transferee furnishes the statement, transmitted a copy of the statement to the chief law enforcement officer of the place of residence of the transferee; and

(ii) (I) five business days (meaning days on which state offices are open) have elapsed from the date the transferor furnished notice of the contents of the statement to the chief law enforcement officer, during which period the transferor has not received information from the chief law enforcement officer that receipt or possession of the handgun by the transferee would be in violation of Federal, State or local law; ...

(C) (I) the transferee has presented to the transferor a permit that ... allows the transferee to possess or acquire a handgun; and ...

(2) A chief law enforcement officer to whom a transferor has provided notice ... shall make a reasonable effort to ascertain within five business days whether receipt or possession would be in violation of the law, including research in whatever State and local recordkeeping systems are available and in a national system designated by the Attorney General.

(8) For purposes of this subsection, the term *chief law enforcement officer* means the chief of police, the sheriff, or an equivalent officer or the designee of any such individual.

(29) The term *handgun* means — ... a firearm which has a short stock and is designed to be held and fired by the use of a single hand; and ... any combination of parts from which a firearm ... can be assembled.

Name _____

# Brady Bill Review

BOB'S GUN SHOP

1. Explain who the "transferor" is described in the Brady Handgun Control bill.

   _____

   _____

2. Explain who the "transferee" is described in the Brady Handgun Control bill.

   _____

   _____

3. Does the bill make it illegal for a person who has a criminal record to buy a handgun?

   Explain your answer. _____

   _____

   _____

4. How long does the law enforcement agency have to check for a criminal record for a per-

   son purchasing a handgun? _____

5. What type of gun does the bill regulate? _____

6. What are the two major points of this bill? _____

   _____

   _____

7. Research to find out who the Brady Bill is named for.

'No Need To Wait To Take A Position On This'

Name _____

# Amendment II

"A well regulated Militia, being necessary to the security of a free State, the right of the people to keep and bear Arms, shall not be infringed."

Study the cartoon, drawn by Tom Engelhardt, and answer the following questions:

1. Who are the two men in the cartoon? _____

   _____

2. The two men in the cartoon are wearing buttons that say NRA GUN LOBBY. Research in the library to find out about the NRA. What does the NRA stand for? _____

   _____

   What is a lobby? _____

   _____

   What does a lobby group do? _____

   _____

3. Why are they shooting at the Brady Bill in the bull's-eye? _____

   _____

4. Explain the cartoon's caption, "No need to wait to take a position on this."

   _____

   _____

5. What is the content of the Brady Bill? _____

   _____

   _____

6. What is the point the cartoonist is making? _____

   _____

   _____

7. What is irony? How is it used in this cartoon? _____

   _____

   _____

Name _____

# Rights Review

Answer the following questions on the back of this sheet of paper:

1. List the five rights protected by the First Amendment.

2. Explain the Establishment Clause and the Exercise Clause.

3. Explain the difference between *belief* and *practice of religion.*

4. What is the clear and present danger test? To which two parts of the First Amendment does it apply?

5. Define *writ.*

6. What four elements are required by the Fourth Amendment before a legal search can be made?

7. Explain the difference between a capital crime and an infamous crime.

8. When an officer arrests a person, the officer must read the accused his "rights." From which amendment is that rule of law derived?

9. Explain what the term *due process of law* means.

10. How many people sit on a grand jury?

Many of the rights guaranteed in the Bill of Rights had their origins in the English Bill of Rights of 1689 and the Declaration of Independence. Match the amendment to the quote from one of those two documents.

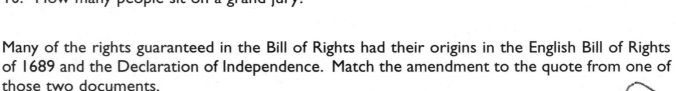

_____ 11. "For transporting us beyond Seas to be tried for pretended offences."

_____ 12. "the subjects, which are protestants, may have arms for their defence."

_____ 13. "quartering large bodies of armed troops among us."

_____ 14. "... petition the Government for a redress of grievances."

_____ 15. "That excessive bail ought not be required nor excessive fines imposed."

A. First

B. Second

C. Third

D. Sixth

E. Eighth

# Bibliography

## Resources for Teachers

Cary, Eve, and Kathleen Willert Peratis. *Woman and the Law*. Lincolnwood, Illinois: National Textbook Company, 1977.

Dumbauld, Edward. *The Bill of Rights and What It Means Today*. Bnorman, Oklahoma: University of Oklahoma, 1957.

Gora, Joel M. *Due Process of Law*. Lincolnwood, Illinois: National Textbook Company, 1977.

Haiman, Franklyn S. *Freedom of Speech*. Lincolnwood, Illinois: National Textbook Company, 1977.

Keller, Clair, and Denny L. Schillings. (Editors). *Teaching About the Constitution*. Washington, DC: National Council for the Social Studies, 1987.

Mason, Alpheus Thomas. *The States Rights Debate-Antifederalism and the Constitution*, Second Edition. New York: Oxford University Press, 1972.

McDonald, Laughlin. *Racial Equality*. Lincolnwood, Illinois: National Textbook Company, 1977.

Padover, Saul K. *The Living U.S. Constitution–Third Revised Edition*. New York: Penguin Books, 1995.

Pfeffer, Leo. *Religious Freedom*. Lincolnwood, Illinois: National Textbook Company, 1977.

Preiss, Byron, and David Osterlund. (Editors). *The Constitution of the United States of America*. New York: Bantam Books, 1987.

Shattuck, John H.F. *Rights of Privacy*. Lincolnwood, Illinois: National Textbook Company, 1977.

Smith, Edward Conrad. *The Constitution of the United States–Eleventh Edition*. New York: Barnes and Noble Books, 1979.

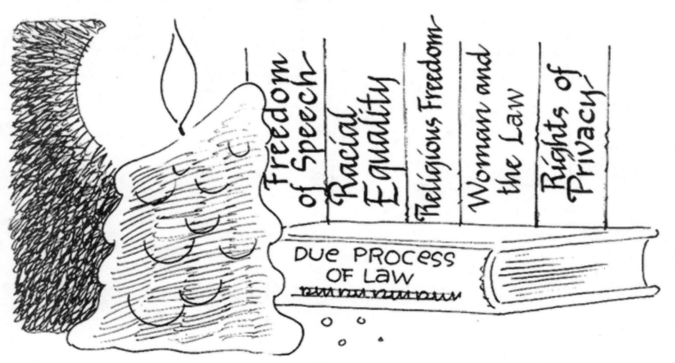

# Bibliography

## Suggested Books for Students

Miers, Earl Schenck. *Documents of Freedom—The Bill of Rights*. New York: Grosset & Dunlap, 1968.

Peterson, Helen Stone. *Give Us Liberty: The Story of the Declaration of Independence*. Champaign, Illinois: Garrard Publishing Company, 1973.

Phelan, Mary Kay. *Our United States Constitution, Created in Convention*. Logan, Iowa: The Perfection Form Company, 1987.

## "The Federal Edifice" Cartoon, page 9

1. states

2. the order of ratification

3. The pillars represent states and are a metaphor for the columns of building (which is a country).

4. a woman who represents freedom, named for Christopher Columbus

5. the reign of Saturn, a mythological Roman god

6. The arts will flourish, agriculture will give her shores divine, commerce will prosper, religion will find a home, the new world will teach the old world endless peace.

7. In favor. Answers will vary.

8. New York and Rhode Island

9. Delaware, New Jersey and Georgia

10. nine

**Trick Question:** Unanimous in convention, though not all delegates signed it; unanimous in that every state ratified it, but not every state vote at state convention was unanimous.

**Bonus Question:** "The Constitution State" because it was the first state to ratify the Constitution.

## Understanding the Events Leading up to the Bill of Rights, page 11

1. George Mason

2. nine

3. yes

4. ARTICLE V–"The Congress, whenever two-thirds of both houses shall deem it necessary, shall propose amendments to this Constitution, or, on the application of the legislatures of two-thirds of the several states, shall call a convention for proposing amendments, which, in either case, shall be valid to all intents and purposes, as part of this Constitution, when ratified by the legislatures of three-fourths of the several states, or by conventions in three-fourths thereof, as the one or the other mode of ratification may be proposed by the Congress; provided that no amendment which may be made prior to the year one thousand eight hundred and eight shall in any manner affect the first and fourth clauses in the ninth section of the first article; and that no state, without its consent, shall be deprived of its equal suffrage in the Senate."

# Answer Key

## Rights Review, page 27

| | | | | |
|---|---|---|---|---|
| 1. 5 | 5. 6 | 9. 2 | 13. 8 | 17. 1 |
| 2. 6 | 6. 1 | 10. 4 | 14. 6 | 18. 6 |
| 3. 1 | 7. 7 | 11. 6 | 15. 3 | 19. 5 |
| 4. 5 | 8. 8 | 12. 1 | 16. 5 | 20. 1 |

## Understanding the Bill of Rights, page 28

1. He has a right to believe in anything he wants. But the Supreme Court has ruled that not all religious practices are legal. The arrest is legal. Though the Constitution protects a person's right to believe in any religion, Congress can legislate to stop certain religious practices. Congress prohibits the practice of polygamy.

2. Yes, they must sell their land. The third clause of the Fifth Amendment states that a person cannot be "deprived of life, liberty, or property be taken for public use without just compensation."

3. No, the actor cannot be tried again because the Fifth Amendment guarantees that no person can "be subject for the same offence to be twice put in jeopardy of life or limb . . . "

4. No, the First Amendment guarantees a person's right to peaceably assemble.

5. It is struck down because it is considered cruel and unusual under the Eighth Amendment.

## Who Said? page 29

1. E. Ninth
2. B. First
3. D. First
4. A. Fourth
5. F. Eighth
6. C. Third

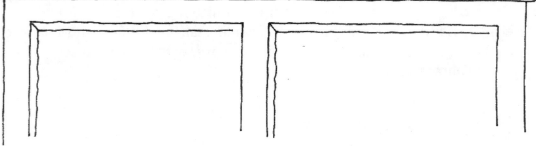

# Answer Key

## Cartoon Quiz, page 33

1. Big.
2. Expensive.
3. Angry.
4. First Amendment upheld.
5. She won.
6. They don't like it; the woman is saying, "there goes the neighborhood."
7. Answers will vary.

## Further Discussion, page 33

Answers will vary. This topic should be discussed in conjunction with "symbolic speech," which has been upheld by the Supreme Court which is why there has been a movement to pass a constitutional amendment to ban flag burning.

## Ladue v. Gilleo Review, page 36

1. They can be regulated by government because of various reasons.
2. It is commonly understood that government can regulate signs because signs can obstruct views, displace land.
3. Sacred, respected.
4. It can influence neighbors.
5. Cheap, convenient, reach neighbors.
6. Third, Fourth.
7. Answers will vary.

## Brady Bill Review, page 39

1. The person selling the gun.
2. The person buying the gun.
3. Yes.
4. Five days.
5. Handgun.
6. Five-day waiting period; national check.

# Answer Key

## Amendment II, page 41

1. NRA lobbyists.
2. National Rifle Association. An organization that promotes a point of view. Tries to influence government to affect legislation.
3. They are shooting at a bill that would put restrictions on handgun purchases.
4. The NRA lobbyists according to this cartoon did not see the contents of the bill before they opposed it.
5. Five-day waiting period; national check.
6. The cartoonist is saying the NRA lobbyists love guns.
7. Irony is a literary device that says one thing when the opposite is true. The legislation is to control guns, and the lobbyists are shooting the bill.

## Rights Review, page 42

1. a. religion, b. speech, c. press, d. assembly, e. redress of grievances.
2. The Establishment Clause prohibits the government from supporting one religion over another. The Exercise Clause protects a person's right to any religious belief.
3. Belief cannot be abridged, but "practice" can be regulated.
4. The clear and present danger test was laid out by the Supreme Court in Schenck v. United States (1919). The court said that speech could be limited if it was shown to present a danger to the community. For example, a man "falsely shouting 'fire' in a theater and causing panic" is not protected by the Free Speech Clause of the First Amendment because the speech caused danger to people pushing their way out of the theater. The clear and present danger test is applied to freedom of speech and freedom of press, both guaranteed in the First Amendment.
5. A legal document authorizing the government to do something.
6. Probable cause, oath, description of a place to be searched, persons or things to be seized.
7. A capital crime, like murder or rape, is punishable by death; an infamous crime is punishable by imprisonment.
8. Fifth.
9. The entire course of law available in the court system.
10. 12 to 23 people.
11. D.
12. B.
13. C.
14. A.
15. E.

**48**